SPRING TIDE

By A K ALAMEDDINE

CONTINUED

CONTINUED

CONTINUED

CONTENTS

CONTINUED

MAIN TITLE FOLLOWED BY CREDITS SEQUENCE

OPEN over a green screen. SUPERIMPOSE in white letters:

<u>SPRING TIDE</u>

FADE IN:

1   EXT. CHARLES RIVER, CAMBRIDGE - MASSACHUSETTS - DAY

It's November. The sun glitters down over the river's water.

1A   CLOSE ON - an upright bicycle is underwater except for

the handlebar, which sticks out like the claws of a scorpion, ready to grab the prey.

1B   IN THE FOREGROUND

A kayaker is approaching, not in the far distance; we close on a BICYCLE HANDLEBAR sticking out of the water.

                    CUT TO:

2   KAYAKER - SAME

2A   The river waves splash on a kayak's hull.

Only the front half of the kayak's frame is in shot. A young man, 18, sits by the stern, athletic and tired from paddling.

2B   WE HEAR A SQUALLING LOUD SCRAPING SOUND of the hull

against metal. The bow rises upward about two inches out of the water and comes to a complete standstill.

  KAYAKER

                        What the, -- ?!

        The noise entices the young man's
        attention. His wary is subtle, but we
        notice. He stops paddling and carefully
        adjusts his body weight to avoid the list.

2C   VIEW ABOVE WATER showing:

        The Kayaker slowly steps forward and reaches
        down, FETCHING UNDER THE WATER SURFACE.
        After a moment, the handlebar of a bicycle
        appears in his view.

        He strains to move it about. It's stuck! Hopeless.

        KAYAKER (CONT'D)

        Oh, for - !

        HE dashes to the stern, grabs the oar,
        and backpaddles, freeing his kayak. He
        looks down over the kayak's side, then
        into the shallow water rippling below
        once more.

3   KAYAKER'S (P.O.V.):

        Notices the scratch on the side of the
        kayak, but way down, he spots a CAR
        SILHOUETTE underwater, on which roof the
        bicycle fastens.

                        CUT TO:

4   EXT. DOVER, MASSACHUSETTS - DAY

5   SUBURBAN - SAME

        WE SEE neatly arranged suburban homes
        outside the city. Some houses are big,
        detached from each other's. Large
        mansions surround the others.

CONTINUED

6   GATED DRIVEWAY - BOUDREAUX'S ESTATE - SAME

           ...a meandering driveway extends from the
           entrance gate to the front of a mansion
           at the end of the drive. Toward the rear
           of the house is...

                                        DISSOLVE TO:

7   EXT. THE GREENHOUSE - DAY

           It's early morning. A well-groomed man,
           mid-60s stands behind a metal rack and
           plants bulbs in clay pots. This is the
           retired Doctor, JACK BOUDREAUX.

7A   ON JACK, his face sweats profusely, he
           steps away from Sun light toward the
           shade.

           Jack checks his watch and walks a few feet to
           the electric panel.

7B   CLOSE ON THE PANEL

           taps the thermostat gauge on the wall. The
           ventilation fan starts running. He heaves a sigh of
           relief.

7C   ON JACK returns to the rack, moves the
           Gardenia pot to a more shaded area,
           prepares the soil, applies fertilizer,
           and mists up his dark Black Roses.

8   INT. MANSION, JACK - THE DEN - DAY

           Jack takes off gloves and apron, gets out
           of the greenhouse door, wipes his slippers,
           and comes to THE DEN. When just he is
           turning the blinds up when the phone rings.
           Jack reaches and then picks up the phone on
           the desk.

                        JACK

CONTINUED

(into phone)

Jack Boudreaux...oh, hello,
ANTHONY...yeah, I'm OK.

9   INT. SHERIFF'S OFFICE - SAME

This is like any other office, flanking
county jail. Anthony DeSosa,60s, a seasoned
police lieutenant detective in DOVER, picks
up the phone receiver.

                    ANTHONY

                    (into

                    phone)

                    Have I caught you at
                    an okay time? Are
                    you available for a
                    minute?
                    INTERCUT:

                         JACK

                    Sure, what's up?

                         ANTHONY

                    I'm afraid ... I
                    don't have good
                    news.

9   ON JACK - SAME

he slides into the leather chair behind the desk.

                         JACK

                    Oh... shoot.

                         ANTHONY

                    THE CHARLES RIVER
                    POLICE found your son
                    STEWART'S body in a
                    car submerged in the
                    RIVER just off the

edge of the BOAT RAMP
near the BOATHOUSE.
His seat belt still
engaged, he is on the
passenger side, and
the car keys are
still in. Every item
recovered from the
car is preserved. Of
course, fingerprints
are not recoverable.

                    JACK

What kind of a car is it?

                    ANTHONY

A small KIA PICANTO with a dirt-
bike still fastened on
its rooftop. As
ominous SCORE plays in
the background... He
Furrows his eyebrows
and looks down,
closing his moist eyes
tight.

                    JACK

          (fighting tears)

Yeah, that's his car. He
kept his body frame slim
and fit. But ...

Stewart went missing
last Christmas. Why
gives?

                    ANTHONY

Correct...but in
that location of
the river and
since then, the

CONTINUED

car must have
dislodged off
the silt on the
river floor.
Yesterday, we
had another full
moon impacting
the Ebb River
current crests at
least nine
feet... The car
must have tilted
by the tidal
current,
exposing the
bicycle
handlebar...a
kayaker has
thumped into it,
noticing the
sunken car, and
called the
TOWNSHIP RIVER
POLICE.

                    JACK
               (tears drip
               down his
               cheeks)
     Wait a moment, Anthony ...
               (wipes
the tears) He then
continues.

                    JACK (CONT'D)
     Are you sure the body
     was Stewart's?

CONTINUED

12   ANTHONY is

        in the

        Police

        office.

                ANTHONY

                The license plate
                owner is Stewart's.
                The VIN number
                indicates the same
                owner -- since

                12   CONTINUED:

                All the car windows
                were stuck in closed,
                the extraction crew
                and the police divers
                had followed the
                protocol and had not
                disturbed the content
                inside the car -- and
                according to the
                coroner, forensic
                study of the DNA
                sample matches that
                observed on Stewart's
                lock of hair that the
                coroner had taken
                from Stewart's house
                and kept in the
                evidence room.

13   ON JACK

        ...more stunned, shaking his head IN DISBELIEF.

CONTINUED

INTERCUT:

14   ON ANTHONY

            in the

            police

            office.

                              ANTHONY

                    So sorry, Jack --
                    let's keep this news
                    between us. I suggest
                    keeping the
                    information
                    confidential. No one
                    should know, perhaps,
                    except your wife and
                    daughter. So sorry for
                    your loss, Doctor;
                    you have my sincere
                    sympathy -- by the
                    way, Stewart's wife,
                    ANNA, is back from
                    Sweden. I do plan to
                    speak with her soon.
                    She has just moved to
                    a new house in BACK
                    BAY. I have her new
                    address ... It was
                    weird that she never
                    filed for a missing
                    person with us, you -
                    did!

                              JACK

                    Yes - that's Anna, the
                    wicked. I hear you.
                    I'll keep her out of
                    the Loop for now.
                    What's her new address?

                              ANTHONY

CONTINUED

26 RIVER STREET. I think
it's OFF MEMORIAL DRIVE, in
CAMBRIDGE.

15   ON JACK

writes down the address on a piece of paper.

                    JACK

        ...I got it. I know
        where that is. Thank
        you for letting me
        know. Please keep in
        touch. So long,
        Anthony.

                    ANTHONY

        Bye-bye, Jack. Again,
        I'm very
        sorry...Yeah, I'll
        call you for any
        updates.

                                        DISSOLVE TO:

16   INT. THE DEN - DAY

Jack covers his face with both hands and sits
quietly in a chair at the back of the desk,
soul-gazing into a faded 8x10 man's portrait,
the most spectacular feature of the room.

17   INSERT - THE PORTRAIT - SAME

it's an old half-length portrait that hangs at
eye level on the wall facing the desk and rests
above a white marble fireplace.

The portrait lights by polished solid brass
lamp that uses two candelabra bulbs. The oval
black parchment shade rests on the mantle. This
man was Jack's father as a young man: a wide
forehead, stern look, big dark black eyes, and
impressive waxed curled mustaches. Without the

CONTINUED

mustaches, the portrait is an uncanny spitting
image of Jack, but forty years younger.

18   INT. THE DEN - SAME

daylight rays flash through the blinds into the
room, revealing all the lavishness around.

Two big bay windows look out into an evergreen
shrub and cropped on the green lawn. A thick
wool rug covers the floor. On a well-assembled
bookshelf lay stacks of books horizontally,
alternating with vertical rows, a lush leather
burgundy lounge chair, and a matching ottoman
in the corner under a lamp shade.

A luxury executive chair is behind a mahogany
desk, struck by only thin slits of sunlight
find their way in. Several faded family photo
memorabilia are on top of the desk and mantle.

19   DAYDREAMING - SAME

Jack now leans back in the chair, hands clasped
behind the head. He glances at family photos. He
recalls his happier time. Eyelids grow gradually
leaden.

He dozes off...

20   INSERT PHOTOS - SAME

On the mantle below the portrait, a stock
of photos can be seen. A photo of a
younger Jack with two young children: a
six-year-old boy, Stewart. A four-year-old
girl, VONY.

And a photo of older Jack with his current wife
CATHY about forty-two. Jack and Cathy had been
married for ten years after the death of his
first wife.

21   REFLECTIONS STOPPED - SAME

his musings are interrupted as he hears
fast footsteps approaching the Den. He

CONTINUED

faintly opens his eyes, looks about,
slightly disturbed, and then catches a
glimpse of Cathy as she rests on one side
of the doorway in an attitude of physical
relaxation.

His eyes grow thoughtful, and glow looking at her
face: a swell woman, straight-forward, she is
tall and wears clear glasses.

22   AT THE DOORWAY - SAME

Cathy watches him, right shoulder leaning on
the wooden doorway. Luscious and healthy dark
blonde hair complements her green eyes. The
dress is a silk slip negligee seethrough
lingerie trimmed with lace.

Cathy holds a cup in one hand and a small
breakfast tray in her other hand. The other
occupant of the room is Jack.

With a small, sweet smile, she greets him in a low,
intimate, playful voice.

                        CATHY

               Good morning, DARLING.
               Did you have a good
               night's sleep? Would
               you like some coffee?
               It is freshly brewed -
               - not too sweet the
               way you like it. I
               also made some FRENCH
               TOASTS with maple
               syrup on top.

                        JACK

               Um... what? Thank
               you, love. Without
               intending, I didn't
               mean to ignore you

CONTINUED

while you were
speaking. You are a
real delight.

Jack is now fully awake. He raises his eyebrows
with a surprised and gratified smile. Cathy looks
back at him.

>   JACK (CONT'D)
>
>   Sorry ... I dozed off
>   while reminiscing about
>   my father in the oil
>   painting. I really miss
>   him.
>
>   CATHY
>
>   I remember you saying
>   that he was the true
>   BOUDREAUX family
>   patriarch. Correct?

CONTINUED

22

                          JACK

                    (contemplating)

          Absolutely. He told me stories
          about how he solved murder cases
          where no one could have...

          A detective by craft, he was
          rigorous in his assessments and
          had grit and valor. He later
          turned into a real estate tycoon
          who built this estate.

Jack considers the top of his desk for a moment, then
looks up.

                          JACK (CONT'D)

          Would you please put all that stuff
          on my desk for now? I'll eat in a
          minute.

                          CATHY

          Yes ... of course, here you go.

Jack extends his hand to grab the coffee cup as Cathy
offers it to him.

                          CATHY (CONT'D)

          Watch out for coffee. It's still hot...

                    (Jack takes a sip)

           By the way, I heard you talking on the
          phone, any news?

                          JACK

That's what I wanted to talk to you about. The Dover police
Lieutenant has just called me. I really don't want to ruin
your day 22   :

                    ... you'd better sit down,
                    sweetheart.

CONTINUED

22

22   :

                              CATHY

                     You got my attention...

She looks about impatiently and sees the low Ottoman.
Drags it closer to the desk as she speaks. Her
delightful face, seen in the light of the room, gives
away a certain troublesome inner fear and deep
distress.

                         CATHY (CONT'D)

                       Please go on --

She modestly covers her exposed thighs with the open
gown. She sits and faces Jack closer.

                              JACK

                There was a decomposed human body found
                inside a car in the Charles River near
                a Boathouse in
                Cambridge. DNA analysis matches
                Stewart's hair sample. The Police
                confirm that the corpse is
                Stewart's.

She shakes her head with deep anguish in her eyes. She
wipes her tears in disbelief.

                              CATHY

                That's horrible! What are you
                going to do?   JACK

                Now we know what his whereabouts
                were. We can now stop wondering.
                But at this point, we must find

22

out what may have happened. God
bless his soul.

                    CATHY

Do they know if it's foul play?

                    JACK

I'm hesitant to say so you don't
get more upset. I know you were
very fond of him, and he cared
very much about you ... the
lieutenant asserts that the Police
declared it as a homicide.
CATHY

Oh! This is awful. He meant so much
to me. Who would want to hurt such
a gentle soul?

                    JACK

That's what we must find out.

                    CATHY

Stewart was supposed to stay with
us last Christmas Eve -- that's
when his wife Anna went to
SWEDEN visiting her parents. Why
do you suppose she waited there
for so long?   JACK

I'm not sure. I heard that she is
now back to work in her
chemistry lab.   CATHY

Do you suppose we should
notify her?   JACK

Absolutely not... not yet; it's too
early. As you know very well, she
has a proclivity for drama. Based
on his brief conversation with
her, the lieutenant warned me
about her state of mind. Besides,

CONTINUED

22

> Anna is not the biggest fan of
> Stewart, anyway.

She raises her eyebrows, opens her eyes, and nods her
head rapidly with enthusiastic agreement.

                    CATHY

> Definitely. I am not sure how
> Stewart got mixed up with a girl
> like her. She is a shady "pick
> me girl" who lured Stewart into
> marriage.

Jack's face distorts with grief -- his eyes shut, his
head begins to nod.

                    JACK (CONT'D)

> After two years of living with her,
> Stewart knew Anna's paranoid
> emotions and whims. She is a heavy
> drinker and smokes like a chimney.
> I could never tell when she could
> suddenly burst into extreme rage.
> She takes tranquilizers --
> Unwittingly, I prescribe them to
> her only when she asks. She always
> needs to pacify her unnatural
> tendency for impulsive anger. My
> thinking was to smooth down her
> fury at home when Stewart was
> around her.

                    CATHY

> Undeniably, she is also an
> unattractive attention seeker --
> with no sense of charm, always a
> nervous wreck.

                    JACK

Right -- she does not know the
fundamental differences between
right and wrong. Though -- she
is an excellent chemist and an
outstanding researcher. She runs
her own research lab with a
special interest in toxic
compounds. Funny -- they dropped
out of sight after Stewart's
went missing! She is on my list
as a suspect.   CATHY

Spare me, this is very
annoying. Let's change the
subject. What's your plan?
JACK

My quest is to find out the truth.
I owe it to my first departed
wife, who bore him. I am not going
to run away from something I must
do. That will be considered an
abdication of my responsibility as
a father.

                Cathy

What do you mean?

                JACK

He was my only son. I must find
out who/or what caused his death.

Cathy rises from her footstool, puts up her hands to
him, holds him, and his head rests on her shoulder.

                CATHY

Darling! You still have his memories.

                JACK

        (softly)

Living with his memories alone
is not enough. You seem

CONTINUED

halfhearted about my ability to
do this job! There is a greater
purpose. There should be
closure, accountability, and
justice --

JACK (CONT'D)

By the way -- Stewart had signed a
five-million-dollar life insurance
when he got married. Anna is the
single beneficiary. But, she has
no right to the death benefit yet
due to the "slayer statute."

CATHY:

What is that?

JACK

The "slayer rule" prevents a life
insurance payout to anyone who
murdered or is closely tied to the
murder of the insured. We still
don't know who murdered Stewart.
Anna has not yet been ruled out as
a suspect.

Jack straightens his posture and rises from his
chair, reaching for the coffee.

JACK (CONT'D)

I must find out by myself. I am
free, and I have a plan, the means,
and the resolve to finish the job.
Oh, did I mention my task for
tomorrow!

Cathy looks over at him with a frown.

CONTINUED

> CATHY
>
> What's tomorrow? What are you
> planning to do? I am worried. What's
> on your mind?

Jack, excited with his newly hatched plan, continues.

> JACK
>
> Tomorrow -- My journey shall
> begin. Enough being confined in the
> greenhouse.   Now
> that I've closed my surgical practice-- I
> start my pursuit at SAINT PETER COLLEGE in
> MANCHESTER, NEW HAMPHIRE. That's where
> Stewart taught Slavic languages for a few
> years. I think I remember his good friend
> ILYA there.   CATHY

> Mm...! Darling, that is
> an old unsolved case.
> YOU ARE not a detective,
> and investigating murder
> is not under your
> purview. We must move on
> with our lives. Why
> don't you leave it to
> the Police to handle it?

> JACK
>
> (tenderly)
>
> Don't be so motherly, Cathy.
> I picked up a lot from my
> father.

Cathy sits quietly. Watching him look over in wonder.
She leaves him with a small smile of approval at his
frankness.

> JACK (CONT'D)

CONTINUED

In all honesty, my old man was a
great detective indeed. I
inherited grit and resolve to
solve emergencies.

                    CATHY

Jack, you are not him. Granted,
you were the bright young surgeon,
and I trust your acumen as a
doctor, but to suddenly decide you
are going to be a detective is
alarming...

                    JACK

              (lightly)

You sound so disapproving,
Cathy?

He looks up sharply with trepidation.

                    JACK (CONT'D)

Remember, I move slowly but
methodically, just like my
dad had done. It is simple, I
need to find out the
perpetrator. Keeping
wondering how he would solve
this case is not helpful. I
have had ample time on my
hands since my retirement. I
am going to pursue this to my
dying day.

                    CATHY

Uh-huh! You can't do it
alone? Let me come along
with you. Please!

                    JACK

CONTINUED

22

> No, I'll be all right. Don't
> be so frightened. I can
> handle it. I am going to
> finish the work I have set
> out to do.

                    CATHY

> Then, why don't we go away on
> vacation for a while? Almost
> ten months have passed, and
> you still haven't been able
> to put the pieces back again.

He considers her offer for a while, then sips his
coffee as he comforts, craving a sweet breakfast
treat.

                    JACK

(gently)

> To forget what happened to my
> son. No way, I will not be
> good company. We will have
> plenty of time together after
> I come back.

> Just be patient.

                    CATHY

> Uh... huh!

Cathy considers his words and finally nods. She is
still worried about his ability to finish the job.
SHE PLOTS a plan.

CONTINUED

DISSOLVE TO:

23   EXT. MANSION, THE PATIO - DAY

Jack steps out of the front door behind Cathy and crosses
to the car parked outside the Garage. The car is a WHITE
CADILLAC. THE HOUSE in the background.

24   ON JACK - SAME

has a recent crew cut, is in a beautifully tailored dark
suit, custom-made shoes, and gives the sense of a man who
savors money and knows how to use it. The collar of a
customized French cuff dress white shirt chafes his neck
lightly, and the pocket square can be seen in the breast
pocket of his jacket complements the black silk String
Tie. He holds a felt Fedora hat.

25   ON CATHY - SAME

is in a light dress, hair combed. She adjusts Jack's neck
collar and necktie. She slides her hands caressing his
cheeks playing about his mouth. After a moment, Jack leans
over and takes Cathy into his arms, kisses her long and
warmly, and holds her body firmly against his with an
intimate embrace, hand still gripping onto the hat's brim.

The kiss is finally interrupted as Jack pulls away enough
smiles while he is ready to put on the hat to cover his
head. There is a quiet moment.

Cathy looks at him long, smiles back reassuringly, places
her hands gently on his arms, and speaks with gentle and
simple sincerity.

Cathy looks surprised at his willingness to continue the
investigation. She initiates the conversation --

                    CATHY

            You look grand!

                    JACK

            Thank you, dear. I'm late...I must
            be on my way, and you must get
            back to the house; it's nippy
            outside.

CONTINUED

DISSOLVE TO:

26 INT/EXT. JACK IN CAR- DAY

Jack Opens the car door, gets in. Cathy steps forward quickly, closing the door behind him.

Jack rolls the window down. Cathy leans down to the window, kisses him lightly, and smiles.

>   JACK

> Thank you, sweetheart. Wish me
> good luck.

Cathy smiles back - unsatisfied. She is quite shaken and realizes Jack put himself in a great deal of trouble and placed himself in unnecessary danger in this foray.

She is anxious, angry, and frustrated at her inability to stop him. As Jack is about to put on his seatbelt, she asks Jack...

>   CATHY

> When will you be back?

>   JACK

> Two to three days at most.

>   CATHY

> Good luck, darling. Don't forget
> to drop off the gift box to your
> granddaughter, little MISSY, at
> your daughter Yvonne's place if
> you have time to visit. Please
> say Hello to both girls and kiss
> them for me. The box is on the
> passenger seat.   JACK

> I won't forget. How can I fail to
> remember? That is Missy's first
> Halloween! I will certainly find
> the time to do that.

CONTINUED

26   CONTINUED:

Jack settles in behind the wheel of his car and slowly
drives off, waving goodbye to Cathy with his arm out the
driver-side window. Cathy watches him go.

27   INT/EXT. JACK'S REAR-VIEW MIRROR - DAY

As he drives, he glances into his rear-view mirror. Cathy
is now further away on the driveway.

Cathy waves back to Jack. Sighs anxiously and murmurs:

                        CATHY

                Good luck...hon. Do you be
                careful, Jack?

We hear her gentle sighs...

                                        DISSOLVE TO:

28   INT/EXT. JACK'S CAR ON THE HIGHWAY - DAY

Jack hits the road. He glances out at his
surroundings.

29   INT/EXT. TRAVELLING ALONG THE FREEWAY - DAY

The colorful Fall foliage of New England is on both sides
of the highway.

30   EXT/INT. JACK'S CAR - DAY

Jack's car dashed along.
He turns off the highway to Interstate 95, NEW HAMPSHIRE
Exit, on his way to MANCHESTER CITY.

                                        DISSOLVE TO:

31   EXT. THE COLLEGE - DAY

A moment later, SAINT PETER College's buildings are
coming into view.

32   Jack arrives at the college stone entrance gate, gets his
            phone out, and makes a short call to Ilya, a college
            faculty member.

            Then turns left, follows the parking sign for visitors,
            uses a short drive, parks the car, and climbs out.

33   EXT. COLLEGE PARKING LOT - CATHY - DAY

            Cathy is in hot pursuit of Jack as soon as his car begins
            to turn into parking. She sits in her black TOYOTA SUV,
            wearing black leather gloves, a wide-brim sun hat, dark
            eyeglasses, and a black leather coat. She reads ELLE
            magazine.

            The car radio is going, and we hear conventional elevator
            music. She is stalking Jack incognito. She glances out
            through her windshield.

34   CATHY'S (P.O.V.)

            a few rows of parked cars. Jack's car is parked near the
            entrance to the Faculty Offices. Beyond it is the main
            door into the building itself.

            There is no activity but for one man who emerges on foot
            and makes his way out -- Walks towards Jack, strolls
            across the courtyard and moves away from the building.

35   INT/EXT. CATHY'S CAR - DAY

            Cathy stays behind the wheel. The face is obstructed by
            the window metal frame and wears a fake black synthetic
            fiber wig. She resumes her reading but does not
            concentrate. Her eyes go back to the courtyard. She
            sees...

36   CATHY'S (P.O.V.)

            ...Jack GETS OUT OF THE CAR, heads up to the Faculty
            Offices, and takes a few strolls outside on his way to get
            there.

CONTINUED

37   EXT. FACULTY BUILDING - DAY

        Standing outside, Jack reads the written motto of the
        College.

38   CLOSE ON A SIGN

        "INITIUM SAPIENTIAL TIMOR DOMINI".

        SUBTITLED: "The fear of the Lord is the beginning of
        Wisdom."

39   EXT. COLLEGE YARD, ILYA - DAY

        The office building is in the backdrop. Jack now paces,
        waiting in front of it. He spots the man who emerged from
        the building is ILYA, 30s, a college roommate and a good
        friend of Stewart, leaving the building and chewing gum.

        Ilya walks towards, then reaches Jack and greets him. Jack
        welcomes him with a Hello and shakes his hand.

                        ILYA

                Hello Doctor Boudreaux, I spotted
                you from my office window on the
                second story upstairs. I can see
                the entire campus yard.

                        JACK

                I was waiting for you in this
                location as agreed to in my
                earlier phone call. I hope I'm not
                interrupting your work. Shall we
                continue the stroll?

        Jack and Ilya are walking together. We walk AHEAD OF THEM.

                        ILYA

                Of course. We're lucky to be
                outside on a beautiful, crisp fall
                day.

CONTINUED

39   CONTINUED:

                    JACK

          The lawn and hedges are perfectly
          manicured. Being a plant man
          myself, I look at them with awe.

                    ILYA

          Yes... I remember your Greenhouse
          while I was paying a visit to
          Stewart two years ago before he
          got married and moved out of the
          house. By the way, I never thanked
          you enough before; you operated on
          me, REMEMBER...

                    JACK

          Yes, Ilya, how can I forget. I
          treated your benign lung tumor.
          How is it going? How do you
          feel? Do you have any breathing
          problems?   ILYA

          No, not at all. I am really doing
          great; I can enjoy my favorite
          pastime - hiking the trails in New
          Hampshire. You might be interested
          to know that I quit smoking on
          your advice. I hope you don't mind
          chewing nicotine gum.

                    JACK

          No. Not too many people can easily quit
          cigarette smoking.

                    ILYA

          Thank you for the compliment...
          What's on your mind, Doctor? Is
          there anything I can do for you?

                    JACK

          Are you still teaching Slavic
          languages at this college?

CONTINUED

39   CONTINUED:

                    Correct? I asked you to come up
                    here, Ilya, knowing that you had
                    taught Russian as my son did.

                              ILYA

                    Yes, I am still. First, sorry to
                    hear about Stewart. We were great
                    friends and shared the same
                    teaching classes. I haven't heard
                    from him for several months, as
                    did the College administration. Do
                    you know his whereabouts yet?

                              JACK

                    That's what I am here for. Stewart
                    was very fond of you, too. I
                    wonder if you can help translate
                    something for me...

Jack retrieves an envelope from the inner Jacket pocket.
In it is a handwritten letter, hands it to Ilya.

                              JACK

                         (continuing)

                    I found this letter hidden in the
                    ticket pocket of Stewart's blazer.
                    It's written in Russian...

                              ILYA

                    Doctor, may I read it.
                    Apparently... Um... Stewart saw
                    your wife Cathy socializing with
                    another man -- VICTOR is his name,
                    a Russian immigrant...

                    Victor and his wife met Cathy
                    in Russia when she was teaching
                    English as a second language.

39 CONTINUED:

                    JACK

          Go on ...Ilya, are there more
          issues that I should know about?

                    ILYA

          Yes, Doctor, there is more --
          Victor is now in the US. He plans
          extortion for money and threatens
          to tarnish Cathy's reputation.
          Especially if Cathy ever revokes
          his immigration sponsorship. He
          also pleads with Cathy to run off
          with him. Last... Victor is
          offended by Stewart. He accuses
          Stewart of ruining his marriage
          and promises to do wrong to him.
          The letter does not mention why.

                    JACK

          Now, I am filled with one more
          heartbreak. I suspected a problem
          when Cathy came home once late,
          smelling cheap men's parfum...by the
          way, can you tell if she is
          rejecting Victor's advances?

Ilya looks at Jack with a shy, embarrassed smile. Then...
sees the wandering look in Jack's eyes, he brightens
quickly...

                    ILYA

          She must have done so because
          Victor is certainly hurt and is
          threatening. He wants her to
          continue with that commitment.
          Doctor, do you think you should
          inform the Police about this
          letter?

CONTINUED

39   CONTINUED:

                         JACK
                    (murmuring)
I'll be the judge of that! But I
Plan for a serious conversation
with Cathy when I return home. So,
apparently my wife is one of the
two sponsors for their immigration
visa. Is that right? Victor and
his wife are the beneficiaries. I
wonder who the second sponsor is?
                         ILYA

Thinking...I just remembered
Stewart talking about sponsoring a
Russian couple. A husband and
wife, and one of them is an
elementary school teacher. I
wonder if that was Victor!

                         JACK

Do we know where Victor lives?

                         ILYA

No...But the letter has a postal
origin in STOCKBRIDGE. I think
that it is in Berkshire. By the
way, Victor's last name is
signed as "ORLOV."
                         JACK

Right... thank you, Ilya. I know
where that is. Berkshire is a
rural region in the mountains of
western Massachusetts.

                         ILYA

Please call me if you have more
questions.

CONTINUED

39   CONTINUED:

                    JACK
          Of course.

:

39   CONTINUED

                    ILYA

               (Shaking hands)

     Also... and forgive the intrusion.
     I do not want to keep this secret
     any longer. A chaotic dispute that
     I inadvertently overheard between
     Stewart and your wife the last
     time I visited him. These
     disagreements may have been
     related to the revelation in this
     letter. Stewart thought that you
     would not be able to wrap your
     mind around such news. That is
     your wife and Victor!

                    JACK

     Cathy and Stewart cared a lot
     about each other. It is a quarrel
     between two family members.

40 CATHY'S (P.O.V.)

     She sees Jack crossing the small courtyard and returns to
     the white Cadillac. He stands for a moment and takes out
     his car keys. He gets in the car and pulls away, leaving
     the campus. He heads for the interstate NH 9 W to
     BERKSHIRE County.

                              DISSOLVE TO:

41   EXT/INT. CATHY'S CAR - DAY

     Cathy tosses the magazine out of the way next to her and
     turns off the radio. She buckles up and starts her car,
     looking intently ahead.

     Through the windshield over the hood of her car. Jack's
     car moves ahead of her.

CONTINUED

She slowly follows, keeping a matched distance, far enough away to see but not to miss Jack's car.

42   EXT/INT. JACK'S CAR - SAME

Jack is behind the wheel and looks ahead, listening to the soundtrack recording like the SIBELIUS Violin Concerto.

DISSOLVE TO:

43   EXT. STOCKBRIDGE, ELEMENTARY SCHOOL YARD - DAY

This is a modest schoolyard. Jack parks the car opposite the school's double doors. He comes out of his car and walks quickly along the pavement toward the main school building and up the steps to the main gateway. It locked. He rings the bell.

44   AT THE SCHOOL MAIN DOOR

we HEAR a woman answering through the door speaker. She inquires as to who he is. Jack declares himself. The woman greets him to come in, and the electric door lock unlocks.

The door opens, and Jack enters.

45   INT. THE SCHOOL'S HALLWAY - DAY

Jack strolls in the main corridor, crosses a female teacher passing the opposite way between classes, and asks her where THE PRINCIPAL'S OFFICE is.

Jack gets the direction toward a small, modest office at the end of that corridor. He gets there by crossing a row of closed classroom doors on each side of the hallway.

Behind these doors, we hear children engaged in reading aloud in their respective classes. Jack goes to the private office door, knocks, and starts to open the door as:

THE PRINCIPAL'VOICE (O.S)

Come in ... the door is open.

CONTINUED

46   THE PRINCIPAL'S OFFICE

The door behind her opens, and Jack enters. THE
PRINCIPAL'S office is in the style of a simple office,
with a small computer on a desk, multiple chairs, large
stack of books stored on a black metallic bookshelf.

46   CONTINUED:

On the walls are some large-framed photographs of awards
certificates with dedications to THE PRINCIPAL.

                         JACK

               Good morning. I am Doctor Jack
               Boudreaux from DOVER.

                    THE PRINCIPAL

               Good morning, Sir. May I help you?
               What are you looking for?

                         JACK

               Do you sign up teachers for the
               Russian language?

                    THE PRINCIPAL

               Yes -- we do.

               This is the only school in
               Berkshire that teaches several
               languages. We have children from
               all over the world.

                         JACK

               I'm looking for Ms. ORLOV,
               one of the teachers. She
               teaches Russian. Does she
               work here? My wife is her US
               immigration sponsor. I would
               like to speak with her...

CONTINUED

The Principal glances at a school staff chart that is
thumb-tacked into a large bulletin board, then looks
down at the roster book on her desk...

                    THE PRINCIPAL
          We have Ms. ORLOV. She is
          blonde, attractive, very
          deep blue eyes, in her 30s -
          - Is that her?

CONTINUED

46   CONTINUED

                    JACK

          I don't know what she looks like,
          because I have never met her
          before.

                    THE PRINCIPAL

          Well... anyhow, since it is an
          important matter, I should
          arrange for you to meet with
          her.

She looks down at the desk. WE SEE her flipping the pages
of the daily teacher's schedule. Then:

                    THE PRINCIPAL

                (continuing)

          Huh - huh... her class ends in a
          few minutes. But the school is
          still in session now. She only
          leaves when school is over for the
          day at noon. I'll let her know,
          though.   But first
          -- may I ask if there are any
          issues with her work visa?

                    JACK

          Not at all. This matter is
          related to her husband, Victor.
          THE PRINCIPAL

          Ms. ORLOV is divorced; you mean
          her ex?

                    JACK

          Sorry, I did not know. Thank you,
          you are very helpful. Please tell
          her to meet me at The NORMAN
          ROCKWELL'S Art Museum. Goodbye
          Mam.

CONTINUED

DISSOLVE TO:

47   INT. INSIDE NORMAN ROCKWELL MUSEUM - DAY

Jack views the gallery one portrait at a time. A woman's silhouette hides behind a column and watches every move of Jack. The woman's profile is the same as the one who followed him to Saint Peter College.

That woman is Cathy with the fake black wig. Another younger woman approaches him and taps him on his shoulder, greeting him with a "Hello." That woman is Ms. Orlov

> JACK
>
> (startled)
>
> He turns around... sorry Mam -
> - do I know you?

> THE WOMAN
>
> She smiles. I'm Ms. ORLOV.

A clean-cut, nice-looking woman, thin and tall, soft-spoken with a cheerful, vigilant manner.

> JACK
>
> Oh... great. Hello, Ms. Orlov. How
> do you do?

He shakes her hand ...

> JACK
>
> (continuing)
>
> My name is Doctor Jack Boudreaux.
> I am glad you came. I have been
> waiting for you. I admire these
> illustrations of Americana. They
> are indeed great pieces of
> history. Thank you for speaking
> with me.

47   CONTINUED

Do you have free time now?

                    Ms. ORLOV

Yes, I do. I know who you are, and
I know why you are here. It is
about Stewart, isn't it not?

                    JACK

But...

                    Ms. ORLOV

A terrific, sweet, and kind
person. Stewart was a
pleasant, gentle, and careful
man. I loved him very much.
He loved me, too. So sorry to
hear that his whereabouts are
still unknown. I've not heard
anything from him since last
Christmas. Stewart supported
me a lot with my immigration
visa...please call me TANYA.

                    JACK

Right..., Tanya. It's about your
ex-husband Victor. Do you know
where he lives or works?

                    TANYA

Somewhere in CAMBRIDGE, MIT. I
think Spectroscopy Laboratory. We
don't talk to each other much any
longer...he is a big and grotesque
man who acts like a mob boss. His
remarks are always inflammatory
and insulting. Victor is an
unpleasant, pompous man, and no
one can even trifle with his
beastly emotions. He always wants
instant gratification.

After the divorce, we both went
our separate ways. The last thing
I know is that he is living with a
girlfriend... one of his students.

CONTINUED

:

47   CONTINUED

Jack flashes a comfortable smile at Tanya and
tries to lead her toward the museum dining
room on the TERRACE...

                    JACK

               (continuing)

          I'm getting hungry. I have not
          eaten lunch yet. I was excited to
          meet with you. We will continue
          this conversation for a moment if
          you find this talk not too
          upsetting. Let's continue the chat
          over lunch. Shall we? It's my
          treat.

                    TANYA

          Yes, I'm starving.

48   INT. THE DINING ROOM, TERRACE - DAY

On the TERRACE, passing over the many well-dressed patrons
until it comes to rest on a table for two dressed against
the far wall.

Jack sits there, dining with Tanya. She is facing him. On
their right side, there is a picture window. Its smaller
frame adds an expansive view. They both are watching the
scenic, natural beauty outside.

While a waiter moves by in the background serving drinks. A
waiter drops the bill on the dining table, and Jack picks
it up. They have just finished their meals. Now, Jack signs
the check. Jack wipes his mouth with a cloth, and he
continues...

                    JACK

          The sea Bass was excellent, and
          the coconut curry sauce was
          delicious. You should have ordered
          the pecan pie. It was tasty. On a
          different note, please go on and

:

talk to me more about this guy,
Victor.

                    TANYA

He is obnoxious, and I get awful
feelings just talking about him --
He is taller and much huskier than
Stewart -- he's built like a MACK
TRUCK. Likes hurting people, too
if they get in his way.
Occasionally violent, has no
concerns about punching or
kicking people. He assaulted me
and engaged in verbal abuse,
often paired with drugs and
alcohol -- he is a very
possessive, egotistic,
narcissistic psychopath. Wants
every woman he sees.
JACK

Did he ever endanger your life?

                    TANYA

Yes...He threatened me, after the
divorce, by killing my family back
in RUSSIA one member at a time
until no one was left. I am still
afraid for my life. I am so glad I
do not have to deal with him any
longer.

                    JACK

Did he ever mention Stewart?

                    TANYA

He hated Stewart and argued a lot
with him.

                    JACK

You don't say! What were their
arguments about?

CONTINUED

:

                TANYA

His conversations with Sewart
always turned into heated squabble
and shouting. I hope you don't get
upset with me if I tell you
something... It may be too
personal.

                JACK

Please do go on.

                TANYA

Stewart knew about Victor's outing
with your wife, Cathy. And asked
Victor to end it and to stay away
from her. Victor continually
refused and warned him not to
interfere.

                JACK

How did you know about all this?

                TANYA

There is usually so much shouting
I overhear the argument. I also
intercepted a letter Victor was
sending to Cathy. So, instead, I
sent it to Stewart to alert him.

                JACK

Well, Tanya, thank you for coming.
We had an interesting discussion
and a good meal. I must meet this
character, Victor, tomorrow to
shed more light on this issue. I
have been driving since early
morning...Is there a good Hotel
around here? I need to rest
overnight.

                TANYA

CONTINUED

:

Yes. About three blocks away, when
you get out of the parking lot,
turn right, then go through the
first traffic light and the HOTEL
will be on your left.

JACK

Thank you again. I appreciated
you talking to me. If there is anything I
can do for you, just let me know. Goodbye.

TANYA

Bye-bye!

DISSOLVE TO:

49   EXT. HOTEL PARKING LOT - DAY

Jack steps out of his car and crosses a large yard of
green grass. Unbeknownst to him Cathy's total plan, yet he
knows that she must have followed him.

49A JACK'S (P.O.V): his eyes search the parking lot slowly but

carefully. Passing over the many cars until it comes to
rest on a car parked against the far wall, a well-
disguised Cathy is seated behind the wheel.

Cathy cannot get a clear look at him. She is turned
slightly away from his direction, there always seems to be
a passing someone to block the view.

But Jack got a clear look at her face when she did turn her
head in his path.

OUT OF (P.O.V): With a smirk on his face, he walks into
the grand lobby of the Hotel and checks in.

50   INT. HOTEL'S SUITE - NIGHT

The darkness of evening comes up. Inside the Hotel room,
Jack looks weary, tired with strain and with hard driving.
His eyes worry, and he is deep in thought. He brushes his
teeth, changes into his pajamas, and crawls into bed.

CONTINUED

:

50   CONTINUED

He sprawls out in awkward attitudes of sleep but snoring
pleasantly. The room overflows with usual hotel furniture,
sofa, table, leather chairs, and artwork. His phone
RINGS... the sound awakes Jack.

He struggles to straighten up, goes to the bedside table
lamp turns on the light. He picks up the phone...

                    JACK

                (on the phone)

          Hello?

                                        INTERCUT:

51   INT. SAME HOTEL - DIFFERENT SUITE - NIGHT

Where the person on Jack's phone line picks up and
answers.

                    CATHY

                (on the phone)

            Hello darling. I hope I
            didn't wake you up.
                    JACK

            Hello sweetheart. I just
            couldn't keep my eyes...
                    CATHY

          You must be exhausted? Your
          impulse to persevere is
          laudable. I'm impressed!
          How're you holding up?

                    JACK

          Just fine. You?

                    CATHY

          The usual -- keeping
          myself busy.
                    JACK

                (low tone)

:

51   CONTINUED

                    Is anything wrong?

          CATHY

               (defensively)

          Of course not! Do I sound as if...
          something's wrong? Am I too
          defensive?

               JACK

               (enjoys her
               responses over
               the line)

          Frankly, maybe!

               CATHY

               I was worried about you. That was
          all. I Was not able to close my eyes to go
          to sleep. So I decided to call you. I
          really need to know where you are heading
          next.   JACK, I'm sorry.

               CATHY

          No need to apologize... Are you
          making any progress?

               JACK

          So far so good, I'm making some
          headway. Tomorrow morning, I am
          going to visit a person at MIT, and
          then in the evening, I'll be
          visiting my daughter, Yvonne, in
          WATERTOWN. Do you still remember
          where that is?

               CATHY

          Yes, of course I do. Don't forget
          to ease the little Missy into
          Halloween for a smooth first
          experience of trick-or-treat...

CONTINUED

:

                         JACK

          Yeah. I'll do that.

                         CATHY

          I'm sure you are tired; I'm going
          to let you sleep. Sorry, I didn't
                    51   CONTINUED

          intend to wake you. Good
          night, hon.   JACK

          Good night, sweetheart.

He realizes Cathy's unmistakable intentions: knowing his next
move because she seems to be awaiting what comes next on his
list. That's okay by him.

          END INTERCUT

                                        DISSOLVE TO:

52   INT. JACK'S HOTEL SUITE - NIGHT

       Jack readies himself for a long drive as soon as the
       Sun rises. He is in bed, out like a light, with warm,
       humorous eyes and a compelling chuckle deep behind
       his eyes. He knows that Cathy is direct to the point
       and tough as nails.

53   INT. THE NEXT MORNING - THE DAY

       Jack checks out, fast leaves the Hotel, and heads for
       his car. He hops in, gets seated comfortably, and
       drives to his next objective...

                                        DISSOLVE TO:

54   EXT. KENDALL SQUARE - CAMBRIDGE - DAY

       ...Jack pulls over to the curb and parks his car on
       treelined Massachusetts Avenue. In the not-too-far
       distance, we see the MAIN MIT BUILDING. Jack gets out
       of the car and walks forward towards it. He remains in
       the foreground.

55   JACK - SAME

          :

steps off the pavement and walks across the street towards the MIT steps.

56   EXT. MIT STEPS - DAY

Jack walks forward and starts up the steps. Enters the main MIT entrance towards the lobby.

CONTINUED

57   INT. MIT - HALLWAY - DAY

         From the lobby, he walks a long hallway. Students are
         going in and out of the administrative offices on both
         sides of this hallway. He stops and pulls to briefly
         study the MIT campus map. It shows the floor plan and
         the department of:

58   SPECTROSCOPY LABORATORY - SAME. After a few hundred
         feet, Jack turns left. Then walks two flights
         downstairs.

         On it in black ink, Mr. Victor Orlov. Jack knocks and
         starts to open the door:

                         A MAN'S VOICE

                         (O.S.)

                  Come in!

         Jack fixes his cufflinks and necktie and enters the
         office. In one corner of the room behind a desk sits a
         man about Stewart's age, mid-30s, rough looking,
         huskily built, slightly balding, with cool, watchful
         eyes. That's Victor. He converses about a Physics
         Project with a much younger woman. She stands opposite
         the desk, listening. Jack enters.

                         JACK

                  Mr. Victor ORLOV, I presume?

                         THE MAN

                  (to Jack) DAH...!

                  I'm.

         Voice laced with a vague Russian accent. Taken
         completely by surprise, staring for a moment into
         Jack's smiling face ...

                         JACK

                  Hello ...I'm Doctor Jack
                  Boudreaux. How do you do?

                         VICTOR

CONTINUED

58   CONTINUED:

> I remember now who you are...
> Stewart's father! I think. Is
> it not?

                    JACK

> Yes... I'm.

                    VICTOR

> What do you want?
> JACK, then you are aware of
> his vanishing last Christmas
> Eve, are you not?

Jack and Victor look at each other for a moment
awkwardly.

                    VICTOR

> Yes? But what is this all about?
> What does it have to do with me?

                    JACK

> I'm running a very narrow and
> factual investigation about that.

                    VICTOR

> What? This is bogus. Ha - ha - ha.

                    JACK
                  (voice firm)

> Please lower your voice! Were
you on good terms with him?
VICTOR Initially, we were, but -

                    JACK

> - I'm set out to find out what
> happened to my son at that
> time...let's cut to the chase: you
> were the last one who saw Stewart
> alive, correct? Did you hurt him
> in any way?

CONTINUED

58   CONTINUED:

> VICTOR
>
> The last time I saw Stewart was in a BISTRO in Cambridge. That was my last encounter with him. Doctor... don't levy this on me. Have you talked to the Police at all?
>
> JACK
>
> Yes... don't change the subject!
>
> VICTOR
>
> Doctor, I'm not dodging your question. It is true, on Christmas then we reconciled. I left him alive! Indeed, I was coercing him not to cancel my immigration visa sponsorship.
>
> JACK
>
> I'm looking at all aspects of the case, and I plan to wrap it up... in my mind, you're a subject of interest in this investigation.
>
> VICTOR
>
> Please don't go down that road, and don't pin this on me! If you are talking about the investigation, I gravely doubt that this allegation is true...I just wanted to spook him a bit to keep him in line. But I calmed down later, as we both acquiesced.
>
> JACK
>
> Is that a fact? I want to get to the bottom of this.
>
> VICTOR

58   CONTINUED:

> **Yeees,!!** We both agreed on a
> workable decision: a fresh start. -
> - I don't know what may have

Happened to him after he left the
bar. It's ludicrous that I'm being
accused of something I did not do.

              JACK

Is that all?

              VICTOR

DAH...this is the truth. I'm
telling you nothing more.

              JACK

Yes, there is. What else...?
Anything related to my wife?

              VICTOR

Nothing happened - I haven't been
makin' it with your wife. Stewart
was outraged about my one-time
outing with her. His request was
to end it. After a short argument,
I coerced him to believe me.

              JACK

Mm...then do you have any
witnesses?

              VICTOR

     Yes, plenty.

     (pointing)

Here is one... my Ph.D. student
was with me that evening. There
were other witnesses, including
restaurant staff and bar manager,
who saw me there.

58   CONTINUED:

                         JACK

              Is that all? You did not stage a
              plan, trickery, or deceit?

                         VICTOR

              You are still badgering me!
              Don't you turn your fire on me?
              That's the whole truth, MAN!
              Now, are you finished?

                         JACK

              This information needs to be
              verified. Now, I need to speak with
              your student.

                         VICTOR

              HELL YES! ... Go ahead. She is
              sitting over there. Her name
              is STEPHANIA.

Jack looks at her and gives her a smile. Victor
searches for his cigarette tin and lighter, finds his
cigarette case, opens it, and checks the lighter.
Turns his head to Jack. Steps forward towards the exit
door...

                         VICTOR

                    (lights his cigarette)

Takes a drag.

                    VICTOR (CONT'D)

                    (blows out clouds)

              I hope I'll never see you again!

                         JACK

              You can go now.

Victor leaves the room in a hurry, slamming the door
shut behind him.

CONTINUED

58   CONTINUED:

Jack turns his attention to Stephania again. STEPHANIA
has light brown hair and black eyes, in the mid-20s,
still stands a few feet away from Jack and faces him.
He regards her coolly and directly for a moment. One
can sense the imperceptible feeling of awkwardness in
his voice ...

                          JACK

          Hello, Ms. STEPHANIA. I hope my
          conversation with Victor will jog
          up your memory.

                          STEPHANIA

          Hello Sir. Yes, it did. I heard
          everything. Victor can be very
          difficult, but he's the best
          Physics teacher I've ever worked
          with. How can I help?

                          JACK

          Well... last Christmas Eve, did you
          witness the meeting between Victor
          and my son Stewart?

                          STEPHANIA

          Yes, I'm aware of that meeting. I
          can't forget what happened. In the
          beginning it was pure chaos and
          misunderstanding. Victor has asked
          to meet him in a Bistro at HARVARD
          SQUARE.

As Stephania starts her tale, that was an unpleasant
experience to recall, but she would stick to the
facts. She began... I remember the encounter took
place last December ... I was outside a Bistro ...

WE FADE IN:

SUPERIMPOSE ON SCREEN - TEN MONTHS EARLIER, FLASH BACK
TO SCENE:

59   INT/EXT. BISTRO - CONTINUOUS - NIGHT

...located on a busy street in Cambridge that is lined
with coffeehouses, independent bookstores, and music
stores. Cars are parked along the curbs. Stephania
parks her car near the corner...

CONTINUED

:

59   CONTINUED

      Inside the car, Stephania checks intently outside through
      her car windshield at people strolling fast on the side
      curb.

      It's cold and snowing.

60   EXT/INT. STEPHANIA'S CAR - NIGHT
      Stephania watches the automated Bistro's GLASS FAÇADE
      DOORS slide open and close. Patrons regulars are going in
      and out. She waits for Victor.

      ...the snow has slowed down considerably. The car's
      windshield fogs up. Stephania rolls down the window, and
      the windshield clears.

61   THROUGH STEPHANIA'S WINDSHIELD - SAME

      Just then as another car parked directly in front of
      Stephania's, she sees a woman having a heated argument
      with a man next to her. Suddenly ... the woman steps out
      of that car and lights a cigarette while she leans on her
      car, looking very angry. Her companion man steps out of
      the car and walks into the Bistro.

62   STEPHANIA - SAME

      At the same time, Stephania spots Victor starting in the
      Bistro. She leaves the car and goes inside the bar. In the
      background, Victor is seated.

63   INT. BAR COUNTERTO AREA - NIGHT

      Victor drinks beer directly from a can. He sips beer,
      followed by crunching peanuts between his teeth...
      Stephania joins him there... Victor punches another beer
      can and hands it to Stephania. From her area, she sees and
      hears everything despite the loud of other patrons
      drinking and laughing.

64   INT. BISTRO CAMBRIDGE - CONTINUOUS - NIGHT

      This man is now inside the bistro. A well-dressed, tidy
      man, complicit, sculpted slim body.

CONTINUED

64   CONTINUED

He gives the sense of a man who appreciates civility. But
deep behind his cool, watchful eyes, an almost
imperceptible annoyance is about to peak.

65   CONTINUED

He glances at the activity that is going on where business
is still rather spirited. There are about a dozen raucous
customers.

He starts crossing the bar. His mellow eyes are quietly
probing, passing over the not-so-well-dressed patrons, the
usual nondescript crowd sitting drinking and chatting
...until they finally come to rest on the person he came
to see. He spots:

66   AT THE BAR, FLAT COUNTERTOP - SAME

...Victor is seated on a tall, padded stool and holds his
drink in his hand, a cigarette is dangling from his mouth.
There are a lot of empty glasses on the bar table. Victor
looks as tired as he feels, his brownish hair disheveled
and dark circles beneath his blazing light brown eyes.

67   THE CONVERSATION - SAME

That man approaches the countertop. He stops, considering
Victor coolly and directly for a while without changing
his expression. There is a quick glimpse of him, a strange
pale face staring back -- they gaze at each beat, and then
Victor takes a drag from his cigarette. The talk escalates
--

                         VICTOR
                       (sitting,
                      gazing up)

          I'm here, Stewart... what's on
            your mind... I can't guess
              what's on your mind.

                        STEWART
                       (standing,
                     gazing down)

CONTINUED

:

66   CONTINUED

>   Keep your guesses to
>   yourself. I had something
>   I wanted to talk about
>   with you.

>   VICTOR

>   Whatever business we have, we
>   can talk over right here.

>   STEWART

>   I asked you to meet me here,
>   Victor, knowing that you had
>   outings with my stepmother,
>   Cathy, but I wonder whether I
>   could persuade you to stop
>   seeing her. She is happily
>   married. Because I know Cathy
>   is a kind person, I will not
>   accept any negative aspersion
>   upon her character.

Victor considers the request for a moment, then looks up
in dismay.

>   VICTOR

>   Is that an order?

>   STEWART Yes!

>   VICTOR

>   I don't like orders. That's
>   what they do in Russia.
>   STEWART
>   (crosses his arms)

>   Look at me when I am talking
>   to you!

:

                    VICTOR
              (shaking head)
      I wouldn't push too far if I were you -
      - Why don't you have a drink?

                    STEWART
      No... no -- thanks, doctor's
      order. I'm in a hurry, Victor.
      What is your answer? I put a fair
      question to you, and I take this
      matter extremely seriously.

66   CONTINUED

      Victor stares at him questioningly, rebuffs the
      question then chuckles.

                    VICTOR
      And if I don't?

                    STEWART
              (eyes rolling)
      I will contact the US immigration
      services to pull your sponsorship.
      You will then be deported back to
      Russia... You don't measure up to
      Cathy. Heed my words and stayed away
      from her. Do I make myself
      abundantly clear?

      During all this wrangling Victor responds, dismissive,
      pointing his finger at Stewart, giving him an angry
      look. Says he doesn't like being marginalized or
      intimidated.

67   STEPHANIA (P.O.V.)

      During all the precede -- Stephania has watched
      intently, while she slowly takes sips of her drink. To
      her, the embattled, grueling insanity between the two
      men continued for a few minutes. Screaming at one
      another, HANDS AND FINGER POINTING AT EACH OTHER.

:

68   OUT OF (P.O.V.), BACK TO SCENE - THE CONVERSATION

The patrons ignore them or shake their heads as if
this is nothing but a usual argument between two
drunken sailors, even though one of them is sober.

69   VICTOR - SAME was irate and lashing out. Berating.
Demanding Stewart not to cancel his sponsorship.
Stewart would ask Victor not to get too touchy and to
acquiesce to his childish fixation with Cathy.

Victor had no choice but to harken to Stewart's
demand, becoming more receptive. He promises to let go
of his teenage obsession with Cathy. That's because

Cathy had made her definite point of rejecting
Victor's advances many times before and for him to
stay clear of her for good.

69   STEWART - SAME

His demeanor looks calmer, changing to a more relaxed
stance and every trace of sadness has turned off. He
shook hands with Victor. After all the squabble, the
silence between them became unbearable! Stewart heads
towards the Bistro's door in a rush.

70   STEPHANIA AND VICTOR - SAME

had witnessed it all. She FINISHES for her drink. Victor
had already finished his. She and Victor start leaving the
bar, just seconds after Stewart had.

                                        DISSOLVE TO:

71   INT/EXT. OUTSIDE BISTRO - NIGHT

A woman waits outside on the sidewalk, standing leaning
on the door of a parked car. We had seen her in a
previous scene.

She wears an outer garment, her face covered with a
hood of a DOWN PARKA for cold weather and smoking a
cigarette.

72   STEWART - SAME

 coffee in hand appears visible in the foreground,
walking behind the door glass. His silhouette is

:

blotted by patrons walking in and out of the bistro.
He steps outside the bistro to give the coffee to that
woman and both enter the car.

                              END FLAHBACK.

SUPERIMPOSED ON THE SCREEN: PRESENT

                              DISSOLVE TO:

74   INT. SPECTROSCOPY OFFICE - MIT- DAY

Once again we see Jack continuing the conversation
with Stephania.

CONTINUED

74   CONTINUED:

                    JACK

     Good God...you certainly heard
     everything. Since your car was just
     in front of that woman's car, did
     you notice the license plate?

                    STEPHANIA

     There was snow mixed with sand and
     muck on the license plate, unable
     to read it. Though... I noticed...
     (rubbing her chin)

     A dirt bicycle fastened on top of
     a small car, KIA. That woman was
     so near my car window that I
     noticed what appeared to be an
     expensive, finely tooled leather
     convertible backpack with
     adjustable straps around her
     shoulders... The initials "JB2AB"
     carved into the unique ornate
     design can be read.

                    JACK

     Please remind me again, what date
     was that?

                    STEPHANIA

     On Christmas Eve -- it was
     snowing lightly by then.

                    JACK

     Are you sure?

                    STEPHANIA

      Yes, I'm certain.

                    JACK

     Fair enough. That's what I
     thought. Thank you, Stephania,

:
you were of great help. Very
illuminating, indeed. All the

CONTINUED

74   CONTINUED

                    (picking up his hat)
           best on your science thesis.
           Goodbye, Miss.

    Jack leaves the office and walks to his car...

                                        DISSOLVE TO:

75   INT/EXT. JACK BRAINSTORMING IN CAR - DAY

    ...Jack sits behind the wheel, collecting his thoughts. He
    eliminates one suspect. Now what? He can't relax, he is a
    person unaccustomed to accepting failure.

    Jack's face now is recording his unease, his fears of
    never finding the perpetrator.

    Suddenly, we hear his murmurs:

                    JACK

           Am I missing something? With
           those initials, I must see
           Anna. She must be a suspect.

    But it's getting late in the afternoon. So Jack decides to
    recalibrate and visit his daughter Vony and her little
    Missy.

    Jack turns the car on. He is on the way to Vony's house,
    which is just half an hour's drive from MIT...

                                        DISSOLVE TO:

76   EXT. VONY'S house, WATERTOWN - HOLLOWEEN - DAY

    Jack stops the car in front of her house, a modest
    suburban home on a quiet, tree-lined street. He is on the
    patio, rings the bell, and lights go on.

77   AT THE PATIO - SAME
Vony, 37, and pretty in a quiet sort of way. She carries a
Halloween basket filled with candy and toys. She puts it on a table
behind the door and then opens the door. She

77   CONTINUED

dresses in a long wool skirt, long-neck sweater, pearl
earrings, and a matching necklace.

Stepping out of her two-story structure house, down the
front walk to the Patio. Her face has a soft glow,
innocent quality, her eyes bright and alive when she
notices Jack standing in front of her, carrying a box...

                    VONY

                (sees her dad)

        Dad !!! What a joyful surprise?

They hugged tightly...

                    VONY

(continuing)

            Come on inside, Dad.

78   INT. INSIDE THE KITCHEN - SAME-DAY

Jack shuts the door behind him. She takes his hat and coat
off and leads him in

...In the KITCHEN a table and two chairs are in evidence.
A highchair for toddlers is in the corner. A tea Kettle is
on the stove.

...Jack places the box at the foot of the table near him.

                    VONY

            Have a seat, Dad. Would you
            like a cup of tea or coffee?

                    JACK

            Yes, tea will be fine, thank
            you. I really need to stay
            awake. It's been a long time

          :
        since we've had tea together.
        That'd be kind of nice.

                    VONY

        Me too!

She picks two clean glasses from the cupboard, picks the
tea kettle off the stove, and fills in the two glasses.
She hands Jack a glass...He takes it. She sits opposite
him.

78   CONTINUED:

                         VONY

                    (continuing)

          Well... I can see you're in good
          health. Do you feel like eating? I
          baked a Pumpkin pie...

Jack Pulls up a chair. Settles in.

                         JACK

          No. Thank you. I never felt
          better, though ...

Draws attention to his stomach.

                         JACK

                    (continuing)

          I keep myself busy working in the
          Greenhouse. Cathy tells me that
          my face is a bit puffier. Do you
          agree?

Vony looks behind his worried face --

                    VONY why do I

          feel you have some

          unpleasant news!

          JACK

          Like your mother, I never doubted
          your intelligence, your
          inquisitiveness. Please sit down
          and drink your tea before it gets
          cold.

                         VONY

78 CONTINUED:

>   Well... you never asked about my
>   little one yet, so I assumed you
>   didn't want her to hear what you
>   were about to tell me. Is that it?
>
>   JACK
>
>   Where is she now?
>
>   VONY
>
>   Next room watching TV.
>
>   JACK
>
>   Good, let's keep her there until I
>   finish my conversation with you. I
>   am afraid a major development has
>   transpired. It is tragic news, I
>   am afraid! Stewart's body has been
>   found. The police declared his
>   death as a homicide. We are all
>   trying to find out why and by
>   whom.

Vony nods her head, the cheeriness of seeing her dad
dissolve in the throes of sorrow. She struggles to hold
back her tears.

Jack takes the handkerchief from his pocket and puts it
over her eyes. He leans forward, gives her a tight hug,
and holds her hands, providing aid for her bereavement.

>   JACK
>
>   (continuing)
>
>   I know how much you cared about
>   your kid, brother. I'm here for you
>   if you need anything.

Vony looks up, overwhelmed, tears running down both
cheeks. She continues to sob. Jack leans over, puts his

CONTINUED

78   CONTINUED:

> arms around her shoulders, and hugs her warmly once
> more.

                    JACK

          We both lost someone that we love.
          He is gone forever. I went through
          this kind of grieves... when your
          mother died, and lately when your
          husband died.

                    VONY

          Yes, I remember -- it was an
          awful time. Now we must go to
          another funeral. Dad, do we know
          who did it and why?

                    JACK

          Unknown! But in large measure,
          progress is being made.

                    VONY

          How're You holding up?

                    JACK

          Well... I'm reaching Out to my
          family ... you and Cathy to share
          my feelings. We will have closure
          once we know who the perpetrator
          is.   VONY

          We still have each other. Isn't
          Dad? Well... what happens now?
          How do we recover?

                    JACK

          Luckily, our survival instinct
          takes over very soon. We must have
          the resolve to endure until the
          shock eases. Hopefully soon.
          Walking it off is also great...

78 CONTINUED:

> Speaking of which, as soon as you
> get dressed, then ask little Missy to come in
> and let her open this box.

He bends down and grabs the box from the
floor, where he has placed it earlier...
JACK

> (continuing)

I'm so anxious to see her, too.

                    VONY

What's in it, Dad?

                    JACK

That's your first Halloween
costume. You were about three, just
the same age as your little one.
Your mother insisted on protecting
this costume all these years for
the grandchildren.

                    VONY

She was very considerate, wasn't
she, Dad?   JACK
Yeah. Indeed she was...

Jack glances at his wristwatch. As they get ready to go
outside, Jack sees little Missy coming out of the TV room.
She looks at him in amazement for a second, realizes he is
her grandpa, and then runs toward him like the wind. He
looks toward her and hurries across the room. As she
reaches him, he opens his arms and hugs her snugly. She
does the same.

                    JACK

(to Missy)

> You're a good hugger.

                    (to VONY)

78   CONTINUED:

                        Oh! Now that she is here, we'd
                        better get going.

79   INT/EXT. VONY'S HOUSE - OUTSIDE STREET - NIGHT

        THE ENSEMBLE JACK, VONY, AND MISSY walk together to the
        front door, out and down the steps, and slowly stroll up
        the street sidewalk.

        Little Missy is in her Halloween costume, holds their
        hands, and walks happily in a casual sort of way in
        between. The snow eases up, but the sky remains grey and
        overcast.

        We see a Jack-o'-lantern glowing brightly on windowsills.
        The neighborhood is filled with CHILDREN dressed in
        Halloween costumes, some carry pumpkins and orange and
        black streamers, some carry Jack-o'-lanterns.

        Several Children in costumes are going door to door
        collecting their treats. Little Missy is as happy as she
        can be, with a bright, wide smile on her face. After a
        while, she collects in her little plastic bag a bunch of
        Halloween candy from trick-or-treating.

        Little Missy is now exhausted. She lifts her arms up in the
        air, a gesture to her mother to carry her. She falls asleep
        on her mother's shoulder, still clasping her treasure bag
        of candy.

        It's completely dark now, and the weather has become
        cooler.

                            JACK

                        (gestures to Vony)

                        I think we should go back
                        home.

80   INT. VONY'S house, WATERTOWN - NIGHT

81   LITTLE MISSY'S BEDROOM

Vony tucks little Missy in bed and kisses her goodnight.

                    LITTLE MISSY

          Good night, Mammy. Good night,
          Grandpa (yells)

                    JACK'S VOICE

               (O.S.)

          Good night, Missy.

82   AT THE PATIO

Vony and Jack are now at the outside doorstep. Jack bids
her goodbye. Vony hugs him in return.

                    VONY

          Dad, I'm glad you passed by. Little
          Missy had the time of her life.
          Please keep me posted.

                    JACK

          I will ... and let me know if you
          need anything. You must get lonely
          living by yourself and a Toddler.
          I don't want to leave you alone
          after the tragic news -- you
          should really consider moving in
          with me and Cathy. You could use
          your old bedroom, which is as you
          had left it. Cathy and I will be
          happy to babysit for you -- Cathy
          and you will have time to catch up
          on things, perhaps go shopping
          together...   VONY

          Dad, I'm happy being alone, but
          will give it a thought.

                    JACK

          One more thing, it's getting late:
          do you mind calling my wife and

CONTINUED

telling her that I'm leaving on my
way to see Anna. After that, I
should be coming home - Tell Cathy
that Anna has recently moved to a
new house at... 28 River STREET
off MEMORIAL DRIVE near the
HARVARD BOATHOUSE.

82   CONTINUED:

Vony marks the address on her phone:

                    VONY

          Got it. So long, Dad. I will
          see you to the door.

                    JACK

              (putting a hat on)

Good night, hon.

83   EXT/INT. JACK IN HIS CAR - NIGHT

Jack drives slowly down MEMORIAL DRIVE towards RIVER
STREET. He looks like he keeps an eye out. Find the
street sign. Gently moves up the street. He murmurs,
"That must be it. Number 26 is over at the end... "What
a dump"!

JACK turns the car into a quiet little residential
street. Pulls up to the driveway. To the entrance steps.
Gets out and shuts the door of the car.

                                        DISSOLVE TO:

84   EXT. ANNA'S HOUSE - BACK BAY - NIGHT

He walks up the walkway. He stops at the porch before
the front door. The house is a middle-income two-story
old BACK BAY house, set back from the street ... that's
Anna's house.

85   AT THE PORCH

Jack stands on the porch, pauses a moment, and glances
up and down the empty street. It's quiet, dark. The

lights are all dark except for a glow from a distant
streetlight.

86   UP THE SIDE WALK

is a series of bushes lining the street. Jack goes up
to the front door he knocks ... there is the sound of
footsteps then the light turns on.

87   AT THE FRONT DOOR - SAME

Anna opens the door and stands in the doorway. She is a
homey blonde in her 30s. She is rather sad about seeing
Jack. She quickly turns her face to hide the fact that she
is unhappy.

                        ANNA

                   (smirk on her
                   face)

              Oh... Jack, please come on in...

88   INT. INSIDE ANNA'S HOUSE - SAME

...Jack wipes his shoes and shakes the snow off his
shoulder and hat. He quickly steps inside and shuts the
door behind him. Enters following Anna.

She strolls through a large living room. She proceeds
towards the half-open door leading to the first-floor
shower room.

A peek at the old shower room shows multiple shower heads
for a rejuvenating hydrotherapy experience...She says.

                        ANNA

                   Ever been in one of these old
                   Cambridge homes?

                        JACK

                   No, I haven't ...Is this where you
                   live?

No answer. Anna bypasses the stairs and slowly makes
her way to the kitchen. Walks through the hallway
between the living room and the kitchen doorway... At
the far end of the hall, then she answers...

CONTINUED

                    ANNA

          You bet. I moved here from
DOVER two weeks ago.
JACK

          Whose house is it?

88   CONTINUED:

        They have now reached...

89   THE KITCHEN

        Anna leads Jack in.

                    ANNA

          ...mine.   Please pull a chair and
          have a seat. How did you get my
          address?

Jack settles in a chair around the kitchen table facing
Anna. He continues:

                    JACK

          From a friend of mine, Anthony
          DeSosa, a police Lieutenant.

Anna turns from him to hide the fact that she is worried.
She wants to change the subject...

                    ANNA

          Want something to drink, Jack?
          There's always hot Coffee and cold
          milk in the fridge. I know you
          don't touch alcohol.

She goes to the corner of the kitchen and comes back in,
wheeling a wicker tea wagon on which are two empty glasses,
a kettle of Turkish tea, and two porcelain stonewares of
sugar and milk.

                    JACK

CONTINUED

No. Thank you, I am rushing back
on my way home before the traffic
builds up.

                    ANNA

I'm glad you are here -- I have
not seen you since last year.

CONTINUED

89   CONTINUED

> But... Jack, what's on your mind --
> why are you here?

                    JACK

> I need to talk to you about
> Stewart! To begin with, do you
> know where Stewart is? Have you
> heard from him?

                    ANNA

> No - Should I have?

Giving him the sort of quick, troubled, disapproving
glance.

                    ANNA

                 (continuing)

> As you know, I was in SWEEDEN over
> Christmas... I haven't heard from
> him, not even a phone call. I
> presume he is still missing.

                    JACK

> Not exactly. When did you last see
> him?

Anna looks agitated, gloomy, and impatiently at him. The
surge of panic and her struggle to contain it is obvious.
She rises, opens the cupboard, picks up an empty glass,
uncorks a half-empty wine bottle, and fills her glass with
the Cabernet.

                    ANNA

> The day before Christmas. That day
> I went to SWEDEN, so I could
> celebrate the Holidays with my
> parents.

CONTINUED

89   CONTINUED:

                        JACK

        Which Airline did you use?

Now in a dour mood. She Holds and shakes the glass of wine
with her hands.

                        ANNA

           It was -- SAS SCANDINAVIAN.

Jack does not change expression, and yet no one can
recognize the feeling of a high point within him and
the almost subtle, small, sarcastic smile deep behind
his eyes. He continues to question dead fast.

                        JACK

        Stop peddling lies! THE LIEUTENANT
        Detective on Stewart's case has
        informed me that your name was
        nowhere to be found on any flight
        manifest. He adjudicated all flight
        departures from BOSTON to STOCKHOLM
        on that day. You must have missed
        your flight?

                        ANNA

        I forgot that I did. Is that so
        bad?

                        JACK

        Did you meet with Stewart that day?

                        ANNA

        Absolutely not!

                        JACK

CONTINUED

89   CONTINUED

          You were the last person who saw
          him alive, wasn't it? Aren't you?
          Please don't insult my
          intelligence. You have already lied
          twice. You have inconsistencies in
          your story. We have a witness who
          saw Stewart in your car on

          Christmas Eve -- the witness also
          noticed the carved letters --
          JB2AB -- writing on your backpack
          that I had given you as a gift. I
          believe it stands for "from Jack
          Boudreaux to Anna Boudreaux" -- of
          course, that is your name. You
          can't sweep this scheme under the
          rug any longer -- By the way, the
          Police found a tiny trace of
          Cyanide detected in Stewart's
          bones. The Cyanide came from the
          same batch of Cyanide crystals
          present in your lab ... anyhow my
          son did not deserve the awful
          decision you took.

Anna's demeanor changes from trembling to NOW FEROCIOUS.
She turns around, hiding her troubled, guilty face. She
has been cornered like a hunted animal...

                    JACK

          (continuing)

          You look frightened. Have I been
          saying something frightening?

Anna pulls a concealed DERINGER from her handbag that she
had placed on a chair near her earlier. She points the gun
at...

CONTINUED

:

                    ANNA

          ...Jack, You'd never know when a
          woman needs to defend herself with
          a small-sized pistol. Stewart
          deserved to die for his despicable,
          degrading comments. I'm never going
          to jail. NEVER EVER!

With a look of horror on his face. Jack stands motionless
for a moment and stares at Anna fearfully. For a moment

CONTINUED

89   CONTINUED   :

both stand still there. And there is total silence... Jack
ponders for a split second.

90   ON JACK'S HANDS
he swiftly slips one hand in his pocket, turns the phone on
and secretly records the conversation. Then Jack speaks.

                    JACK

                    I don't think you want to start
                    any shooting, Anna... Some people
                    know I'm now meeting with you.

Anna looks at him without saying anything, but the gun

doesn't lower.

                    ANNA

                    Get up -- and let's go to
                    your car. Remember, I have a
                    gun.

91   AT THE FRONT DOOR

by this time, both are on their feet, leaving the kitchen.
She moves a few steps behind Jack. She flicks the front
door lights off. She leads him to the back door, and he
leads her to his car.

Outside, it is dark except for lights from distant
houses. Jack looks back at her, a slight frown on his
face. His eyes study her intently as he says:

                    JACK

                    Sure...It will be tragic if
                    this gun goes off...

CONTINUED

91   CONTINUED

                    ANNA

          I know what I'm doing. Just keep
          going in front of me a bit faster
          ...Don't do anything funny, or I
          will shoot...

They both dash along to...

                              DISSOLVE TO:

92   EXT/INT. JACK'S CAR - NIGHT

      Jack is in the driver's seat, starts the motor, and
      pulls the car out of the driveway.
      JACK

                    Where to -- Anna?

Anna is in the passenger seat, gun poised at Jack.

                    ANNA

          This is a dead-end street. So slow
          down and prowl over to the curbside
          of the street, then stop and shut
          the light and engine off.

Jack follows her instructions carefully. They are both
silent in the car for just a moment. Then...

                    JACK

          GOOD ENOUGH...Please stop
          trembling, or the gun might go
          off.

He tries to force himself to relax and almost succeeds
when he is sprung to tension again by the thought of his
son's death.

CONTINUED

:

92   CONTINUED

                              JACK

                           (continuing)

               Tell me whatever happened after
               your meeting with Stewart.

                              ANNA

               I think this is your last wish, so
               I'm happy to oblige...

Anna's VOICE: continuing from the previous scene.

                           ANNA(V.O.)

                           (O.S.)

          On Christmas Eve, I drove Stewart to a Bistro in
          Cambridge for a brief meeting with a man called Victor
          Orlov...

                                           FLASHBACK TO:

93   EXT. BISTRO, CAMBRIDGE - NIGHT (TEN MONTHS EARLIER)

          ONCE AGAIN, we are back at the Bistro.

          It's a cold December evening.

          WE SEE: light snow coming down.

          Anna's voice continues speaking as we see the Bistro as a
          one-story structure serving food and wine. It's Bistro all
          the way and not to be confused with a quiet mom-and-pop
          restaurant.

94   INT/EXT. STEWART'S CAR - NIGHT

:

A parked car near the curb outside the Bistro. We see Anna in the DRIVER seat. She glances at the bistro.

95   ANNA'S (P.O.V)

Stewart gets out through the front two sliding doors of the bar carrying two cups of hot coffee. He approaches the car.

CONTINUED

96   OUT OF (P.O.V.)...

Anna opens her side window. Stewart hands her the cups.

He goes around the car, gets in, shuts the door, and sits
back behind the wheel.

97   INSERT CUP HOLDER

Anna places his cup of coffee in the car's cup holder. Anna
holds her cup in her trembling hand. She thanks him then...

                          ANNA

                     (sips coffee)

                  ...I want to discuss our marriage
                  before I go on my long trip to
                  SWEEDEN. We are no longer
                  intimate. A long time since you
                  last touched me. And you have
                  never been at home much lately.
                  Are you seeing someone else?

                          STEWART

                     (hesitantly)

                  Yes-I'm...in love with someone
                  else. Specifically a Russian
                  schoolteacher. We love each other
                  very much. We plan to get married.

                          ANNA

                  Do you think I don't love you
                  anymore, is that it?

                          STEWART

                  That... is not the point.

98   BACK IN JACK'SCAR (INTERCUT) - Anna continues with a

            disconnected voice...

                          ANNA

                     (to JACK)

CONTINUED

                :

                He said awful things to me...
                like ...I was too big, ugly,   98
                CONTINUED

                always whining, drinking,
                smoking, on tranquilizers,
                and worse... that I should
                never have been born! I
                thought that covered
                everything. I was pondering
                for a moment then he said ...

99   BACK IN STEWART'S CAR - (INTERCUT)

                         STEWART

                      (hesitant)

                Honestly,... I want a divorce.

                         ANNA

                What are you doing, Stewart?
                What are you doing? You're
                not LEAVING ME.

100   IN JACK'S CAR - Anna is fighting tears as she continues.
                         ANNA

                      (to JACK)

                It wasn't a lover's quarrel.
                It was rather a "goodbye
                girl" and thank you, Mam, for
                everything -- Hearing all
                these appalling things about
                me and the end of my
                marriage, I was demoralized.
                That is the end of my
                endurance -- I start shaking
                incessantly, so I must calm
                down. I asked him to go back

CONTINUED

:

to the restaurant and get me
a small bottle of mull wine
so I could relax on my red-
eye trip overseas -- I
mentioned

continuing the discussion at
home in a more private
setting. He said the time is
here, and now, that is final.
In a moment of overwhelming
rampage while, he went back to
the bistro to get me wine...

101   ANNA'S (P.O.V): As soon as Stewart enters the bistro,
Anna quickly reaches for her purse and picks up from
it and:

102   CLOSE - AN ENVELOPE WITH A LABEL

It reads: TOXIC HYDROCYANATIC ACID combined with
Aconite Alkaloid.

103   OUT OF (P.O.V.) - BACK IN JACK'S CAR, Anna
continues:

ANNA

(to Jack)

The mixture resembles
granulated sugar and
dissolves in water just as
well as sugar does -- These
toxic chemicals represent a
specific area of my grants-
supported research -- Early
data from my lab shows that
the combination would delay
the cyanide's immediate
lethal effect.
JACK

What did you do with the envelop
content?

CONTINUED

:

104   CONTINUED

                    ANNA

          I poured in Jack's coffee, a
          scant amount of that.

          Concoction -- again to delay
          his certain death for a bit.

                    JACK

               (shakes his head)

What happened then?

                    ANNA

          Stewart starts small, sipping
          his coffee. After a few sips
          of coffee, he complains of a
          headache. He convulses, stops
          breathing... slumping over
          PULSENESS ...dead -

                    JACK

               (cuts in, furious,
               loud)

          - GOOD GOD WOMAN!?...DID
          YOU start CPR?

                    ANNA

          He died earlier than I
          expected...perhaps because of
          his slender figure.

                    JACK

          You gave him the wrong dose.
          Is that it? I call it a
          BLOODY MURDER. How did he end
          up in the river?

CONTINUED

　　　　　　　　　：

　　Anna continues to remember the following events that
follow the death of Stewart - FAST SEQUENCES MONTAGE - 105   -
ANNA (P.O.V.):

　　　　- She is behind the wheel. She turned the engine on,
　　　　　pulled off the curb, and drove away from potential
　　　　　peering people's eyes walking in droves and in single
　　　　　on the sidewalk of that street...

CONTINUED

- Not knowing what to do, she drove the car as fast as she could to the...

- BOAT RAMP IN CAMBRIDGE - NIGHT

- Anna parks the car at the edge of the Charles River.

- Anna puts the gear selector in neutral.

- She gets out of the car after leaving the door open. - She leaned into the car and started to push it.

- The front of the car began to roll down the ramp slowly, then quickly into the river.

- She jumps away, slamming the door shut.

- The car fills quickly with water and sinks. Immediately through thin ice with Stewart's body in it.

106   OUT OF (P.O.V.) - when the last scene fades

(END MONTAGE).

107   INT/EXT. BACK IN JACK'S CAR - NIGHT - INTERCUT

During all of this, Anna's face relaxes a tad, BUT her hand trembles. She still points the gun at Jack. The car now stands near a bush, away from the clearing under a big tree. A real look of anguish comes into Jack's face:

                    JACK

                (raged)

            YOU'RE FAR LESS PERSPICOUS THAN I
            THOUGHT!

Anna looks at him in near panic, menacing. And Anna studies it, then speaks.

                    ANNA

            All right... Get out of the car,
            keep your hands up so I can see

CONTINUED

107   CONTINUED:

       them. I remind you no sudden move,
or I will shoot.

The engine and lights are off. The area becomes a twilight
zone...

                JACK

     And again, be careful with that gun.
     Any shaking -

                ANNA

      (interrupting)

     - Get out of the car and stand near
     the bush. Turn around and face the
     tree... Sorry Jack ...

Jack nods and starts walking along. Turns his face to
Anna to talk to her a bit more... to find a way out of
his dilemma... his eyes are caught by the bush in the
corner outside Anna's vision:

                JACK

     I don't want you to be sorry.
     Stay cool now, Anna. Don't be
     reckless. Most people manage
     their guns responsibly...

      (softly)

     You did it, and you got
     caught! One murder is enough!
     Don't make things harder for
     you? It's your own fault, and
     I'm the one who really feels
     sorry for you.

Panic fears rush his mind. Does not want to antagonize her
further, but he is compelled to continue talking. He can do
nothing else, feeling like a shooting target.

CONTINUED

107   CONTINUED:

Fights to find a way out of his deadly encounter. There is
no way out...While this is underway, Anna is so distraught
and still watches him flaming with resolution. Her
intentions are unmistakable.

Anna looks down at him with a hatred that is almost ready
to explode... READY TO FIRE.

                    JACK

        Can't we just settle this?
        Otherwise...

                    ANNA

        Otherwise what? What are you going
        to do about it? You're ranting too
        much!

        No use? I have a gun. What's
        stopping me? Is there any other
        way? I didn't come here to argue.

                    JACK

        Otherwise -- you will be facing
        serious consequences.

        Your situation is already serious.

        Whatever you are thinking of
        doing, please don't do it before
        you get in any deeper...

Anna slowly looks uncaring at him with a striking
coldness.

                    ANNA

        So long,

Jack...

There is a brief silence.

108   ON JACK glares in terror at Anna.
        Faces her with wide eye whites, the
        skin between the two eyebrows wrinkles
        briefly, listening with mounting fear.

109   THE MOON is out partially now.

        Jack glances once more at the darkened area about two feet
        in the vicinity of Anna, lit only by the narrow light rays
        from the moon spilling in. To Jack, this is a flash second
        of diversion from panic to inquisitiveness. His prying eyes
        now center on the bush.

109   ON THE BUSH

        begins to come alive, something is moving, then reappears
        closer as the moonlight flashes.

110   ON A DARK FIGURE

        emerges SUDDENLY. We don't see the shape of the face, just
        the lower body. Hurriedly, the figure walks toward Anna. We
        can barely make out. In the twilight dimness the shape
        becomes more and more clear...

111   ON CATHY

        we see a disguised Cathy with a BLACKENED face like a SWAT
        officer. From a unique perch she digests what she
        sees...then she seems to appear from nowhere... Cathy
        reaches in through the bushes, picks up an old wooden canoe
        oar off the ground, and swiftly lunges at Anna.

                        CATHY

                Why you criminal minded --!

112   ON ANNA

        startled, she suddenly stops, and turns back toward
        the mystery dark shape, staring at the bushes behind
        her.

113   ON JACK

        unexpectedly, he almost with a gasp, glad yet
        uncertain if he sees Cathy.

114   THE FIGHT - SAME - NIGHT

CONTINUED

Cathy instinctively strikes Anna with the oar. The
blow lands on Anna's arm with a sharp CRACK.

115   ON ANNA

screams a high, piercing shriek...

116   ON CATHY

                    CATHY

          Take this -- "you some
          bloodthirsty UNSCRUPULOUS
          psycho" --!

118   CATHY'S (P.O.V.)
the attack throws Anna off balance. A gunshot is heard. The
gun flings to the ground. The shot went off in Jack's
direction but left him unscathed. He breathes a sigh of
relief. Jack looks at Anna with a grin but seizes the
moment and races to the gun. He picks it up.

119   OUT OF (P.O.V.) BACK TO SCENE - THE FIGHT - NIGHT

120   ON ANNA

astounded, Anna staggers a step forward, trying to gather
herself.

121   ON CATHY

  Suddenly, Cathy strikes a second charge on the back of
Anna's shoulders, this time by a mighty blow.

122   ON THE OLD OAR

breaks into pieces.

123   ON ANNA

now stumbles to stay upright. Cathy gripped Anna's hair and
slung her to the ground backward. Anna repels off, then
plummets, sprawling on the ground.

124   ON Cathy

is about to clobber Anna once more, aiming it right at
Anna's abdomen.

When Jack suddenly just looks at her intervening:

                    JACK

CONTINUED

> That's enough, dear. She has no
> fight left in her.

125   EXT. BUSH NEAR BOATHOUSE, CAMBRIDGE - NIGHT Cathy takes off
her wig and eyeglasses.

> CATHY
>
> That was ugly and you were
> wonderful, dear. When that
> gun was on you, Jack, I
> thought you were a goner.

Jack sees and hears her voice, realizing that she is indeed
Cathy.

> JACK
>
> Happy to see you, dear. You
> did a commendable job.

He bends over, Checking Anna's neck for a palpable pulse.
Finds one...

> JACK
>
> Cathy -- Anna is still alive
> and breathing. Great news, I
> am calling the Police.

> CATHY
>
> Yeah -- you do that.

126   EXT. THE CALL - NIGHT

Jack pulls out his phone from his pocket and dials...

> JACK
>
> (on the phone)
>
> This is Doctor Jack Boudreaux,

CONTINUED

126   CONTINUED:

> Detective Anthony, please --
>
> > (listens)
>
> Hello Anthony...Cathy and I are
> near the boathouse...
>
> > (listens)
>
> Been just fine, thanks.
>
> > (listens)
>
> Yes, yes, both of us... Stop
> Worrying...
>
> > (waits)
>
> Yes. Believe me. We have
> the murder...   (waits)
>
> It was Anna. I have her admission
> recorded on my phone.
>
> > (Waits)
>
> Yes -- yes, she is alive. She
> needs an ambulance, though...
>
> > (listens)
>
> We just... had to stop her...We'll
> be going home soon.
>
> > (listens)
>
> Right, right, yes?... No, it's all
> right; I'll call you back. Yes.
> Yes! I'll call you... Me too.
> Goodbye, Anthony.

127   ON JACK AND CATHY

Jack taps the end call button on the phone, steps toward
Cathy. During the preceding, Cathy still attends to daze
Anna helps to prop up Anna's head and keeps her
comfortable.

CONTINUED

127   CONTINUED:

                              CATHY
                        (to Jack)
                  Are the Police coming?

                              JACK
                  Yes. They will be here shortly.

127   CONTINUED:

                              CATHY
                  How are you feeling?

                              JACK
                  Better. I was scared... I couldn't
                  do much.

                              CATHY
                  You did enough, Jack. As usual, at
                  times of crisis, you are cool and
                  levelheaded.

                              JACK
                  But it was all you...

                              CATHY
                  I was protecting my beloved
                  husband. I worried about you, so I
                  followed every move you made since
                  you left home for New Hampshire.
                  You certainly met my expectations.

            Jack gleams with radiant, wide-opened eyes, beaming.

                              JACK

127   CONTINUED:

Glad to see you Dear, but what
took you so long? I started to get
anxious.

                    CATHY

Vony gave me Anna's address as
you instructed her. That was very
helpful to find this dreadful
place. But Anna's home is set
back off the street, too dark and
hard to find. The street sign is
also hidden behind hanging tree
branches --

                    JACK

I know that -- I also know
that you had been following me
all along my trip.
CATHY

          (surprised)

I was surprised. I thought I was
well disguised!

                    JACK

Never mind... I am glad you came
along after all, dear! I liked
being chased by a beautiful woman.
I think I began to like this job.

I think I can do it.

                    CATHY

I knew you could, Jack. I knew it
just as well as anything.

                    JACK

But you kept me out of
harm's way...
CATHY

CONTINUED

Don't say anything more. Just hold
me tight.

As she stands there, his face close to hers. She takes him
in her arms. They embrace.

128   EXT. MOMENT AFTER THE FIGHT - NIGHT

We now hear the sirens of police and wailing ambulance
trailing fire engines. Police squad cars and ambulances
dash toward the scene.

Dismounted motorcycle cops turn off the road and place
"keep out" warning signs with yellow tape. They stand
directing the

CONTINUED

128   CONTINUED

now small car traffic and one or two onlookers down the
general street.

JACK

(tiredly)

Finally, the law is here.

(relieved)

That is a relief. We are both
tired, I am ready to
collapse, let's go home.

CATHY

Great idea.

DISSOLVE TO:

129   INT. MANSION, DINING ROOM - NIGHT

Jack and Cathy are lovingly looking at each other. A real
ROMANTIC CANDLELIGHT DINNER. IN THE MIDDLE OF THE TABLE
STANDS A VASE WITH FLOWERS. THE SOFT FLICKERING GLOW OF
SCENTED CANDLES MAKES THE RELAXED AMBIENCE EVEN MORE
SEDUCTIVE.

Jack's eyebrows raise a little. Likewise, the corners of
the mouth lift a tad with his cheeks.

JACK

Hon, this is a crucial moment in our lives. It's time to
have a conversation about us. I don't want to second
guess what I'm feeling. My dream came true when I
married you. Honestly ... I don't know much about women,
they make me nervous. You are a woman of extraordinary
courage, poise, and understanding...I understand you,
and I like what I 129   CONTINUED.

understand, and I couldn't have done
this without you. I think you are

CONTINUED

129   CONTINUED.

>   Terrific, mighty easy on the eyes,
            regal, and you take my breath away.

                    CATHY

            This is the nicest thing anyone
            ever said to me. I have never been
            as joyful in my life. You have
            certainly proved your prowess at a
            time of imminent danger. If you
            are brand to stay, I will stay
            with you. Living with you is a
            privilege any woman would cherish.

                    JACK

        Thank you, sweetheart...

                    (gently)

            Cathy -- I have been waiting for a
            time like this for a long time...
            What have you done? What was that
            all about with Victor? What did
            you see in that guy anyway? Let's
            not throw all this away.

                    CATHY

            I want to apologize for not
            telling you sooner.
            Please forgive me, Jack
            (hesitant). You were never home!
            Busy with your practice. I had
            the impression that you loved
            your patients more than me! So,
            I did not want to be cooped up
            at home.

                    (remorseful)

I knew Victor when I was in RUSSIA I just meant to spend some time

outside the house. But -- this guy
wanted more to be intimate

exactly. I couldn't believe it. I
thought he was just a friend -- I
told him that I love my husband,
and we will have a lot of problems
since we are so different. It's
time to let go, and we're never
going to meet up again.

JACK

Now I understand.

He picks up a beautiful gift box that he had earlier
hidden under the table. Unwrap a bouquet of roses.

JACK

(continuing)

Here is a small token of my
appreciation. I've never thanked
you enough for saving my life.
These dark roses ARE REALLY,
REALLY DIFFICULT TO BREED. I
collected from the greenhouse -
Sweety... stand with me.

CATHY

Hon -- I will always be right here
in good grace with you. Our love was
put to the test, but we do not
believe in defeat. Do we, Jack?

JACK

(in good spirits)

You have my sincere gratitude. ARE
YOU FREE SATURDAY NIGHT? We're
dancing at Hyatt Spinnaker in
CAMBRIDGE.

CONTINUED

:

                    CATHY

I'm free. When should I get ready?

                    JACK

The dinner is at eight. The dance
is at ten.

CONTINUED

:

DISSOLVE TO:

130   EXT. DRIVEWAY - DAY (The next morning)

Jack returns from the Police station and proceeds to
the car into the driveway, stopping at the steps of the
mansion's porch entrance. He gets out, shuts the car
door, and goes up the steps. Jack clears his shoes,
reaches the entrance door, and opens it.

131   INT. STAIRCASE, MANSION - DAY

Jack enters the main house and crosses the hall...

                    JACK

          Hon - I'm home!

He looks up and ascends to the first few steps of the
grand staircase. From the upper landing comes the sound
of delight, Cathy. She starts down the staircase. As he
slowly moves up the stairs, Cathy reaches him in the
middle of the staircase. She stretches out her arms.
They embrace. They take solace in each other's arms.

                    CATHY

          I missed you already. How did it
          go at the Police station?

                    JACK

          I missed you too, dear. It has all
          worked out well, and I signed my
          statement at the station. The
          investigation is still active,
          though the Police got the
          specifics, including the recording
          on my phone. Taken in totality,
          proves Anna's guilt.

                    CATHY: You have

documented the scuffle?

                    JACK

          Yes!

CONTINUED

:

131   CONTINUED:

                         CATHY

          Why am I not surprised? How about
          Anna?

                         JACK

          She was discharged from the
          Hospital's emergency room.
          Initially, facing overwhelming
          evidence, she was catatonic. She
          has recovered since -- except
          for a minor headache...

          She has partially cooperated with
          the police. She certainly gave one
          absurdity after another.

                         CATHY

          What did the Police do?

                         JACK

          Considering her jarring, jaw-
          dropping testimony, the Police
          held her in jail awaiting her
          trial. According to Anthony,
          Anna is formally charged with
          one count of first-degree
          murder. There are other pending
          charges. If convicted, she will
          get a life sentence without the
          possibility of Parole.

                         CATHY

          She will never see the light

of day!

JACK   Right...

          By the way...I'm all for this
          job! It requires patience and
          temperance and a lot of sweating
          out... though dangerous, it's.....

CONTINUED

131   CONTINUED:

> Only fun. Nothing would thrill me
> more -- if it were possible.

                    CATHY

> What do you mean?

                    JACK

> BOSTON LIFE INSURANCE had
> requested me to investigate this
> case from the very beginning.
>
> I had accepted!
>
> Now the payment is released to
> my entire family as the
> beneficiary for Stewart's life
> insurance policy. Anna is out
> of the picture for good...On
> that basis, BOSTON LIFE is
> asking me for future jobs as a
> special national "Private
> Investigator" AT LARGE for the
> company.

                    CATHY

> That is wonderful news.
>
> Can I be of help, too?

                    JACK

> We'll see.

Jack hears a lot of commotion outside and leaves to find
out. Cathy smiles to herself.

                                        DISSOLVE TO:

132   EXT. MANSION'S PATIO - DAY

Jack finds Anthony waiting outside. Two police officers, a
handful of newspaper reporters and photographers, and

132   CONTINUED:

a mobile unit truck from the local television outlet
have jumped out of the cars.

Some are running up to Jack and Anthony, and others in
larger groups have already huddled around them.

                    JACK

               (to Anthony)

          It's like a three-ring circus here.

          Let me drive you back to the
          Police station.

                    ANTHONY

          Thank you. That's a good
          idea. I agree it's too raucous here.

133   EXT/INT. JACK'S CAR - DAY
        Jack sits behind the wheel, pulls out, and continues
        slowly on the driveway. Anthony is in the passenger
        seat.

                    ANTHONY

               (wide smile)

          You finally wrapped up this case
          in a nice bow.   JACK

          Contemptible, Anna finally
          showed her real color. She is
          the coldest snake I have ever
          dealt with. There is a context
          to her action, which is her
          wickedness.

                    ANTHONY

That's right. Thanks to you. What she did cannot be justified in

133   CONTINUED:

> any form or shape... You might be
> interested to know that she lost
> her chemist license.

After a moment, during which we see through the
windshield in the short distance, utility people are all
over the place, and public works trucks and red cones
are in place.

Jack sees Two cops directing the traffic-- Jack slows
down.

Anthony rolls down the window, looks out and up, and
gazes at the green street sign...

                        ANTHONY

                Hold it here, Jack!

Jack puts the brakes on and looks at him for a flicker
of a moment. Astonished, Anthony studies the sign for a
flash. He sees...

134   ANTHONY'S (P.O.V.)

WE GLANCE from inside the car and TRACK THE CONSTRUCTION
SITE

We are at the gate. City Street maintenance workers
affix a new roadside sign: "CATHERINE DR.", replacing
the old sign "HYBRIS WAY."

135   OUT OF (P.O.V.) - BACK TO SCENE.

                        ANTHONY

                OH, Jack, I never really noticed
                that this lane was called HYBRIS
                WAY. Who was HYBRIS?

                          JACK

135   CONTINUED:

                    HYBRIS was Anna's maiden name.
                    Dover Parish Council approves my
                    request to replace the Driveway
                    sign. Anna's character traits of
                    impulsive, outrageous behavior
                    can be summarized by the term
                    'hybris' —- In ancient GREECE,
                    HYBRIS was the goddess of
                    insolence, reckless pride, and…

                    Arrogance. As someone said, "If
                    you hate the people who dislike
                    you, you lose." —- It's
                    delightful to see that the sign
                    has now been changed. It's now
                    named in honor of my wife,
                    Cathy.

136   INT. MANSION - NIGHT (SATURDAY)

It's eleven o'clock. Cathy and Jack each joyfully
continue with married life adventure, a delightful
outing with dinner and dancing. Each feels happy,
secure, and satisfied. This romantic atmosphere does not
last long. Jack's phone RINGS...

                          JACK
              Excuse me, darling...

He pulls the phone from his pocket.

                     JACK ON PHONE
Hello?

                                    INTERCUT AS REQUIRED:

                                              CONTINUED

137   A MAN FROM BOSTON LIFE

                    MAN'S VOICE
              (O.S.)

     Hello Doctor. This is life in Boston.

                    JACK

     I hope you have a good reason for
     calling me so late at night.

                    MAN'S VOICE
              (O.S.)

     We have another case for you to
     participate in. Are you willing
     to take it?   JACK

          (on the phone)

     Sir, please hold on for a
     minute...

Jack looks at Cathy. Eyebrows and eyelids pulled up
together. He wonders. Asks for permission. Cathy signals
back to him and whispers:

                    CATHY

     Only if we do it together!

                    JACK

          (on the phone)

     Thank you for holding. Of
     course, I will take it. Please
     go on with the specifics of this
     case...

END INTERCUT.

CONTINUED

FADE

OUT

WE MOVE EXTREMELY CLOSE TOWARD Jack's face.
When his profile fills the GREEN SCREEN
showing the printed words "SPRING TIDE,"
Jack gives us a wink -- AS WE ROLL END
CREDIS

                    THE END

www.ingramcontent.com/pod-product-compliance
Lightning Source LLC
Chambersburg PA
CBHW081658270326
41933CB00017B/3205